dream rooms

create and customize
UNLIMITED
virtual bedrooms!

Always check with an adult before making permanent changes to anything in your real bedroom (such as adding stickers to a lampshade or using fabric paint to decorate a pillowcase). And if you're not sure how to do something, ask an adult for help before you start. After all, every interior designer needs an assistant!

Written by Rennie Brown
Illustrated by Stevie Hale-Jones

First published by Parragon in 2008
Parragon
Queen Street House
4 Queen Street
Bath BA1 1HE, UK

ISBN 978-1-4054-9586-8

Manufactured in China
Please retain this information for future reference

dream rooms

PaRragon

Bath · New York · Singapore · Hong Kong · Cologne · Delhi · Melbourne

how it works

Installing and running your CD-ROM

These pages are bursting with ideas for your dream bedroom designs! Use the book for inspiration, then follow the instructions below and get designing with your CD-ROM!

Using a PC:

1. Put the CD into the CD drive.
2. Double-click on "My Computer."
3. Double-click on the CD drive icon "Dream Rooms."
4. Double-click on the "start_pc" icon. You will see a loading icon and your CD will start.

Using an Apple Mac:

1. Put the CD into the CD drive.
2. Double-click on the CD drive icon "Dream Rooms."
3. Double-click on the "start_mac" icon. You will see a loading icon and your CD will start.

System requirements

Apple Mac:

OSX
- ❋ Power Macintosh G4 500 MHz or higher
- ❋ Running a minimum Mac OS X 10.2.6, 10.3, 10.4
- ❋ CD-ROM drive
- ❋ Sound card
- ❋ Monitor displaying at least
  1024 x 768 pixels in 256 colors

PC:

- ❋ WINDOWS 98 / 2000 / ME / XP / Vista
- ❋ Pentium IV processor
- ❋ CD-ROM drive
- ❋ Sound card
- ❋ Monitor displaying at least 1024 x 768
  pixels in 256 colours or higher
- ❋ 256 MB of RAM (512 MB recommended)

Top Tip
Once you've installed your
CD-ROM, you're all ready to go!
If you get stuck, just click the
"Help" button on the screen.

designer's guide

Furniture style

When it comes to choosing furniture, a girl's gotta go with her heart! Pick whatever suits your mood and you won't go wrong!

Fabulous themes

Give your bedroom a fabulous theme! You could go for fairytale fashion, fresh and funky, chill-out classic, or warm and cozy—it's up to you!

Amazing accessories

Accessories show the world what you're all about, so get ready to go wild with pictures, posters, and knick-knacks!

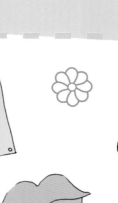

What's up?

Click through the Finish Your Room section of the CD-ROM to set your dream room up for a party, a sleepover, or a chilled-out afternoon!

Top Tip
Experiment with styles and colors until you've gotten the look you want!

furniture shop

Beds

Are you ready to design your ultimate dream room? Picking the right bed and bedside table is the first step! Make a style statement or go plain and accessorize later. It's all up to you!

Sweet dreams

When you're designing a whole new bedroom, choosing a bed is a good place to start! Decide what kind of look you want, then pick a bed to suit your mood!

Look at the dreamy canopy and pretty ironwork on this beautiful bedstead. It's fit for a princess!

Feeling kind of funky? Go for a retro bed like this. It's a total design statement!

A natural wood bedstead with a heart-shaped motif is country farmhouse chic!

Real Rooms
It's totally easy to change the look of your own bed by using different duvet covers and throws!

Check out this barred headboard if you want a timeless classic.

A modern chunky bed in moulded plastic looks seriously twenty-first century.

furniture shop
Chairs and tables

Choose a bedside table to complement your bed, then pick a cool desk or cute vanity to complete your set of bedroom furniture. Just make sure that your dream furniture fits your dream lifestyle!

Bedside tables

What would a girl do without her bedside table? They're the perfect place to keep books, diaries, and other secret stuff! Choose carefully!

The soft, curved shape of this oval bedside table would look gorgeous in any room!

A squared-off bedside table in natural wood is simple and classy.

Desks and vanities

If you're the type of glammed-up girl who's into makeup and fashion, your dream room totally needs a vanity. Or if you're more into creative stuff like writing, painting, or crafts, pick a cute desk to do it on.

This natural wood desk would suit a creative girl who loves to paint. Are you the arty type?

Calling all starlets! The superstar lights on this vanity will totally steal the show!

Real Rooms
Personalize a chair in your room with some cool pillows in your favorite color!

choosing a theme

Can't decide on a theme for your room? Don't panic! This cool quiz will reveal a fabulous theme to suit your mood!

I can't stop daydreaming today!

Yes

No

I feel like relaxing today.

No

yes

I want to dance to my favorite CD.

yes

No

I feel like dressing in bright clothes.

No

I can't wait to curl up with my new book.

yes

No

I'm in the mood for a girlie gossip.

yes

No

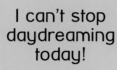
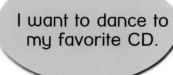

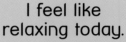

Fairytale Fashion

yes

I secretly wish I was a princess.

No

Fresh and Funky

No

Chill-out Classic

I feel like wearing a big baggy sweater.

yes

Warm and Cozy

fabulous themes

Fairytale fashion

WHAT'S THE STYLE?
Fairytale style can be as magical and girlie as you like!

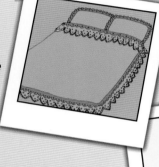

WHO DOES IT SUIT?
Sweet daydreamers

THEME ESSENTIALS: Look out for enchanting lacy fabrics, beautifully made pillows and curtains, and anything that sparkles and shines!

Fresh and funky

WHAT'S THE STYLE?
The funky look is bold, bright, and urban.

THEME ESSENTIALS:
Loads of loud colors, graphic patterns, and prints. Cool ethnic details and anything inspired by music!

WHO DOES IT SUIT?
Rock chicks

14

Warm and cozy

WHAT'S THE STYLE?
This theme is the ultimate in snug chic!

THEME ESSENTIALS:
Loads of soft and fluffy fabrics, and floor pillows. Cute vintage prints and anything inspired by the country.

WHO DOES IT SUIT?
Stay-at-home honeys

Chill-out classic

THEME ESSENTIALS: Cool colors, natural fabrics and materials, like eco-friendly wood and organic cotton. Prints and designs inspired by Japan.

WHAT'S THE STYLE?
Simple designs with a few carefully chosen details.

WHO DOES IT SUIT?
Eco-babes

Top Tip
Try out the themes on the CD-ROM first, then try mixing and matching items from the different sections!

fabulous themes

Fairytale fashion

Fairytale fashion is gorgeous and girlie! Let your inner princess go wild and create a fashionable room fit for royalty!

Walls and floors

Choosing walls and floors for your fairytale room will give the room a whole new look. Now's your chance to get girlie!

These fairytale flagstones will make any room feel like an enchanted palace!

This gorgeous castle mural is perfect for romantic daydreamers.

Cute coverings

Now it's time to get girlie with duvets and quilts! Go for beautiful fabrics or pretty prints!

This beautiful satin quilt is just the thing for a princess in training!

Any girl would have sweet dreams with this pretty fairy on her duvet!

Finishing touches

Add a sprinkle of magic to your fairytale room with the prettiest curtains and rugs in the land!

This sweetheart rug would add a touch of romance to any room!

These curtains are as pretty as a picture. Will you choose them to frame your window?

Check out the bows on those curtains!

Real Rooms

Why not make some cool star decorations for your own bedroom? Just draw the shapes on colored paper and cut them out!

An elaborate molding around the wall is palace-style!

Wrought-iron bedside table

Satin bedspread with loads of detail

fabulous themes

Fresh and funky

Get the fresh and funky look with a mix of urban designs, cool retro styles, and ethnic details.

Walls and floors

Funky rooms are all about edgy, urban designs. Walls and floors need to make a statement—it's all about the wow factor!

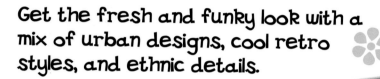

A tiled floor in a funky pattern is ultra-stylish.

This attention-grabbing mural screams urban chic. Can your walls handle it?

Cute coverings

Forget pastel colors and shy styles. If you want a funky bed you've got to think big and bold!

Crank up the volume with this funky set. Rock chicks will love it!

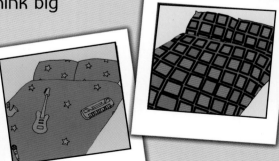

This brightly colored set is totally retro! Are you ready to make a style statement?

Finishing touches

If you want a totally fresh and funky room, choose finishing touches with hard-hitting designs.

The funky abstract design on this rug gives it a fresh and edgy vibe.

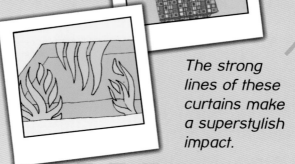

The strong lines of these curtains make a superstylish impact.

You'll feel like you're in a New York loft apartment with exposed brickwork like this.

Real Rooms

Jazz up your dull old light switch by adding glittery stickers.

Futuristic bedside table

Retro detail

Bold colors

fabulous themes

Warm and cozy

Sometimes a girl just wants to cuddle up and get cozy! Follow your heart to create the perfect place to relax.

Walls and floors

Add warmth and texture to your walls and floors with heart-warming colors and traditional designs.

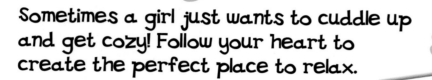

This pure wool carpet is so soft and springy—it's like a hug for your feet!

Get that glowing feeling with this gorgeous sunset mural—it's the coziest picture ever!

Cute coverings

Now it's time to make your bed as cozy as can be! Go for supersoft fabrics and beautiful colors.

Country girls will love the flowers and birds on this lovely bedspread.

Would you like to snuggle up under this pretty patchwork quilt?

Finishing touches

It's the little things that make a room feel cozy, so look for pretty designs and anything soft and cuddly!

Home-loving girls will fall in love with this totally fluffy rug!

These velvet curtains would make a gorgeous frame for any window!

Natural wood furniture

Real Rooms

Use a handful of multicolored yarn or long, thin strips of tulle in different colors to tie back your curtains.

THE GYPSY PUNKS

Rich colors

Fluffy rug

Soft carpet

fabulous themes

Chill-out classic

Make your dream bedroom into the ultimate chill-out zone, with natural patterns and soothing colors.

Walls and floors

Forget fussy designs and hectic colors! Get the chilled-out vibe with pure and simple walls and floors.

This simple wooden screen would give your dream room a truly relaxing vibe.

Get back to nature with this calming leaf border. It's perfect for chilled-out chicks.

Cute coverings

Get in the zone with calming colors! Keep it pure and simple and go for bedspreads in natural shades!

Chilled-out chicks will love this cool Japanese print!

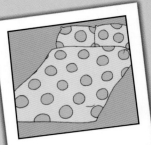

These gorgeous polka dots give this duvet set a totally fresh vibe.

Finishing touches

Turn your dream room into a haven of calm by mixing plain designs with simple shapes and natural colors.

The simple graphic shapes on this rug are classic chill-out.

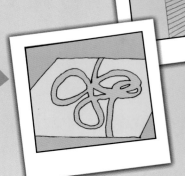

These Venetian blinds would let the sunshine stream into your dream room!

Just because a chick's chilled-out doesn't mean she can't be glam as well!

Real Rooms

Use a pack of stickers to decorate a plain lampshade and wastepaper basket and turn them into a matching set.

Simple and stylish bed

Natural fiber rug

amazing accessories

Make it yours!

Now that you've chosen a theme for your room, it's time to get personal! Pick out accessories that fit with your dream room and your dream hobbies! It's all about you and what you like!

Sweet dreamers will love this Native American feathery dream catcher.

A bulletin board is a great place for pinning up little notes and photos.

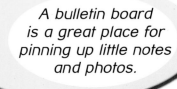

Fresh flowers are superstylish!

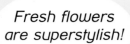

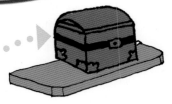

All girls need a place to keep their precious things! How about this cute keepsake box?

Real Rooms

Drape a pretty scarf over the top of a picture frame or across the headboard of your bed.

No self-respecting rock chick would be without her music posters!

Urban girls will go wild for this funky skyline.

These tasseled pillows would add instant chic to any girl's room!

hanging out!

What's next?

Is your room perfect for a party, a sleepover, or a chilled-out afternoon? Click through the activities on the CD-ROM and pick what you'd like to do right now!

Crank up the volume for the coolest dance party with all your friends!

It can be your birthday every day of the year with these birthday girl balloons!

Watch all your favorite TV shows and movies on your own top-of-the-range flatscreen TV.

Are you ready to rock out? Practise your band's latest songs on this funky guitar.

Lose yourself in the latest book by your fave author!

Love girlie gossip and giggles? Have a sleepover with your best friends!

This cute little kitten loves your dream room. Will you let her stay the night?

If you're into sophisticated snacks these are the nibbles for you!

Top Tip
Want to make some funky invitations? Add some party fun to your CD-ROM bedroom and use print-outs as invitations!

Real Rooms
Show the world what you're about! Use colored tissue paper to create a hobby-themed picture for your bedroom window.

designer's tips

Get inspired!

Top interior designers are always looking out for new ideas they can use in their rooms. It could be an amazing color combo, a new fabric, or an inspirational piece of furniture.

Why not make a collection of your favorite colors and patterns by drawing them in your sketchbook? Interior designers use this technique to help them work out the best color combos!

chill out fabrics

funky fabrics

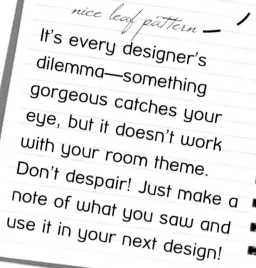

nice leaf pattern

It's every designer's dilemma—something gorgeous catches your eye, but it doesn't work with your room theme. Don't despair! Just make a note of what you saw and use it in your next design!

Top Tip
Tuck a mini notepad in your bag, so you can make design notes on the move!

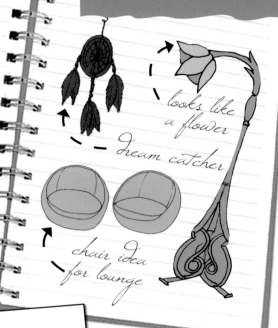

looks like a flower

dream catcher

chair idea for lounge

glass bricks

heart cushions

simple bedcover

Star style!
Test your creative skills by designing a dream bedroom for your fave popstar! You could even pick a color scheme that goes with their latest outfit!

funky rug

floor lamp

get real

Make it happen!

You've designed your dream room on screen, now bring it to life with these supercool crafts! Are you ready to get creative?

You don't have to have loads of cash to be like a princess! Make a canopy for your own bed by hanging a length of floaty material from your ceiling. Wow!

Design a cool door sign based on your favorite hobby. Choose something simple like a riding hat or some ballet shoes, write your name underneath, and hang it on your door handle!

Paint a simple flower design on a giant piece of paper to create a stunning and original wall decoration.

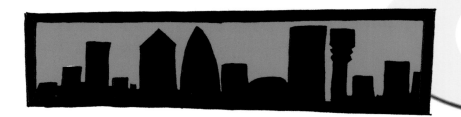

Make a funky cityscape by cutting some building shapes out of black paper and sticking them onto a bright cardstock background.

Use fabric paint to decorate a solid-colored pillowcase. This dreamy cloud design is really easy to paint and it looks totally gorgeous!

designer's tips

Design library

You can design as many virtual bedrooms as you like using your CD-ROM. Keep a record of them all and create a design library that you can use for inspiration.

Top Tip

When you've finished designing, you can either print out your dream room or save it as a jpeg. If you experience any problems printing directly from the CD-ROM, try saving your dream room as a jpeg, then printing it out from your chosen image application.